HOW TO BE INTERNET FAMOUS

THE #1 SOCIAL MEDIA MARKETING BOOK ON 'HOW TO GO VIRAL' AND BUILD A POWERFUL PERSONAL BRAND FOR SOCIAL MEDIA INFLUENCERS

How To Be Internet Famous

CONTENTS

Part One Social Media Basics...................................... **3**

    1. Figure Out Your Why 5

    2. Pick Your Niche......................................7

    3. Decide on Your Focus Platforms...........9

    4. Be Consistent..11

    5. Hack The Hashtags................................13

    6. Do Followers Even Matter 15

Part Two How To Go Viral **17**

    7. Value, Value, Value 19

    8. Stop Doing What Everyone Else is Doing..........23

    9. Comments Mean More Than You Think...........27

    10. Trigger One Of The Three Types of Emotional Experiences 31

    11. Keep Up With Social Media Trends.................35

    12. Keywords Matter 37

    13. Short & Sweet is Better........................39

Part Three How To Become "Famous" **41**

    14. Defining "Fame" 43

    15. Know Everyone and Their Mother 45

    16. Ask For Advice and Feedback...........47

How To Be Internet Famous

17. Diversify Your Income..49

18. Work Harder Than Everyone Else....................51

19. Learn How To Adapt..53

20. It's Not Rocket Science...55

Part Four Monetizing Your Reach 57

21. Followers Don't Equate to Money.....................59

22. Make Brands Want You.......................................61

23. Don't Promote Garbage......................................63

24. Know Your Worth...67

25. Ways To Monetize..69

26. Don't Overthink It...85

Acknowledgments 86

If you are reading this book, I assume you are a wannabe social media influencer or an established creator looking to grow your following. The future of advertising is through social media so there is no better time than NOW to build a brand around yourself.

A little background on me: My name is Brendan Cox and over the past 5 years, I've worked behind the scenes for a variety of influencers and brands of all kinds. From working with dating start-ups to clothing brands and micro-influencers to celebrities I've seen it all.

I've worked on numerous campaigns where creators get paid $20,000 for a 15 second Tik Tok post. At that rate, they are making about $18,000,000 an hour. Well not really - but you get the point. Being an influencer can be lucrative.

Although I have no desire to be in the spotlight I know exactly what it takes to get the spotlight put on you. This book is going to break down everything I know about virality on the internet.

First things first, understand that overnight success IS real on the internet. When I say success I mean views and virality, not necessarily monetary success, although that too is possible. This is why being an influencer is so volatile. You can post 1 video and overnight have 10 million views and be trending worldwide. BUT, at the same time, you can do something stupid and lose your platform overnight. So pick your shots and choose your words wisely as the stakes are high.

PART ONE

SOCIAL MEDIA BASICS

Brendan Cox

CHAPTER 1
FIGURE OUT YOUR WHY

"If you can't figure out your purpose, figure out your passion. For your passion will lead you right into your purpose." — *T.D. Jakes.*

Everyone wants to be a social media influencer these days. When I mean everyone, go ask a class of middle schoolers (or even high schoolers) what they want to be when they grow up and 90% of them say they want to be a Tik Toker or a YouTuber within seconds. But why? What's the big draw of becoming an influencer? Is it the money? The free food? The luxurious lifestyles? What is the draw...

Well if you're in it for any of those three reasons, you're in it for the wrong reasons. Find a WHY that is around something you are passionate about. If you have been dancing your entire life and it's a passion of yours, dancing on Tik Tok could be for you. If you're into cars, make car videos on YouTube.

What's so amazing about being an influencer is you can create content around ANYTHING (and I mean anything) and if you are creative enough, you will grow a following.

Take Milad Mirg for example. He's a creator on the internet with millions of followers and billions of views across his various platforms. Milad started on Tik Tok creating content around his job at Subway® where he'd film himself making sandwiches while storytelling over his videos. Now - Mirg has earned millions (I'm guessing... but remember I know this space) and built a personal brand like no other. If Milad can become a millionaire by creating unique content around his job at Subway® you can create content around literally ANYTHING.

Just remember: social media is a lot easier of a "job" when you are making content around something you genuinely enjoy.

CHAPTER 2
PICK YOUR NICHE

"Build a business around your passion otherwise it won't last. Money will always follow when you are doing something you genuinely enjoy." – Brendan Cox

Stop chasing the money and start chasing something you are passionate about when picking your niche. Of course, certain niches are more profitable than others but being an "influencer" is no fun when your influence is regarding something that you could care less about.

- If you like horses: build a brand around you and your horse

- If you like art: showcase your art to the internet in a unique way

- If you like acting: show off your acting skills through POV videos online

- If you like sports: make over-the-top sports highlight videos

My point is, the internet is so broad and there are so many different types of people on it. To build a brand around something you DON'T like would just be silly. People are interested in everything so find your niche and the people interested in that niche will eventually find you (of course if you are creating good content.)

CHAPTER 3
DECIDE ON YOUR FOCUS PLATFORMS

"It is those who concentrate on but one thing at a time who advance in this world." - Og Mandino

As an influencer, it's tough to try to NOT do it all, especially when you see the most successful content creators creating content on every platform. When you're just starting, don't try to do everything because you'll end up half-assing everything. Instead, do ONE thing WELL.

For example, if your goal is to be a YouTuber when you first start go ALL IN on YouTube. Put Tik Tok, Twitter, and Instagram on the back burner and put all your energy into making the BEST possible YouTube content.

When you diverge your time and energy between multiple platforms you'll start to notice the quality of your content go down (until of course you have the funds to hire a team and start to outsource some of your editings and work to freelancers)

Brendan Cox

CHAPTER 4
BE CONSISTENT

"Success isn't always about greatness. It's about consistency. Consistent hard work leads to success. Greatness will come." - Dwayne Johnson

If you want to be a successful influencer, consistency is by far the MOST important trait you must have. There are very few influencers who posted a couple of videos or pictures and became famous within a week or so. Everyone has posted videos where they spent hours creating something they thought was going to do well and flopped. BUT, you need to push through.

Consistency on social media shows persistence and builds momentum around your brand. Being consistent forms unbreakable habits that will make social media become second nature (especially when creating something you genuinely enjoy).

If you are building a personal brand around something you are truly passionate about, it shouldn't be all about the initial views and followers. If you CONSISTENTLY create AMAZING (yes, amazing, not half-assed, rushed content) you will succeed on social media. To reach that follower milestone or get that first brand deal, it will require consistent effort to push toward whatever that goal may be.

CHAPTER 5
HACK THE HASHTAGS

What the hell is a hashtag? Everyone has seen one or scrolled past one but what is their actual purpose on the internet? Hashtags are labels used on almost every social media platform that make it easier to discover information within a certain niche or topic. Hashtags essentially encourage social media users to categorize their information so the algorithm can best feed other users information they might be interested in.

Think about it. When you scroll on the Instagram explore page, it's usually pretty spot-on in feeding you content that you are likely to engage with or share with a friend.

When using hashtags I highly recommend using the hashtag pyramid strategy. Using this strategy will put you in the best shape for being favored by algorithms. It essentially takes different size hashtags, some being broader than others, and putting them all together to form one hashtag set.

How many hashtags should you use? This answer varies heavily by platform. I'd worry less about how many hashtags you use and worry more about WHAT hashtags you use.

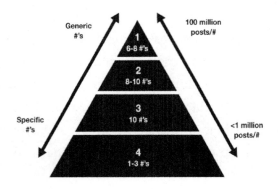

CHAPTER 6
DO FOLLOWERS EVEN MATTER

When it comes to monetizing your audience, do followers matter? NO, not necessarily. If you bought 100,000 followers and get 3 likes per post, brands will not work with you. In this space having a loyal audience that engages with your content is much more important than having a certain number of followers.

Let's talk about buying followers for a second. Buying followers is the WORST possible thing you can do as an influencer. Not just because the followers aren't real (and you have fake clout) but because it will forever damage your potential reach on social platforms. When you have 100,000 followers and only a few of them are real, that means your content is getting sent out to thousands of bots and none of them are viewing, liking, sharing, or engaging in your content. What's the problem with that? Well since the people that follow you don't even engage in your content, why would Instagram push it out to their explore page for others to see? Or Tik Tok's For You page. The answer is they won't. Moral of the story: DO NOT BUY FOLLOWERS. EVER.

Remember, just because you have 5,000 or 10,000 followers doesn't mean you can't make serious money. Having a smaller following around a super-profitable niche can honestly be a gold mine. The most important thing is curating a heavily engaged audience around a niche topic so advertisers know exactly what your followers are interested in.

PART TWO

HOW TO GO VIRAL

Brendan Cox

CHAPTER 7
VALUE, VALUE, VALUE

"Try first to be a man of value; success will follow." - Albert Einstein

Ok now that the boring stuff is OVER, here's where we get into the juiciness of gaining viral traction online.

I'm not here to waste any of your time, so I'm going to keep this short and to the point. Regardless of which social media platform you go on, virality directly correlates to value, always, always, always. When I say value, that doesn't always mean educational value. Providing the user on the other end of the screen value can be seen in terms of entertainment, educational, or often comedic value. But regardless, something valueless doesn't have a chance of going viral.

Let's break down the three types of value-adds on the internet:

Entertainment Value: This type of value is often seen in skits, movies, television shows, and so on. Keeping the end-user hooked because they are entertained is one way to drive up your watch time and have that user share a photo or video to a friend or family member in awe of being entertained by it.

Educational Value: Educational value is becoming more and more prominent on social media. Whether this is directly educating your audience through an appealing infographic or an educational video, you are giving your audience knowledge.

Comedic Value: If the person consuming your content is "laughing out loud" then you are providing them comedic value. Comedic value is the most common way of obtaining viral success on social platforms as videos that offer this type of value are also most likely to be shared.

Now of course it seems like anything can be of value. Since if a 15-year-old boy can go viral for dancing on Tik Tok, can't anything? What's the best way to gauge if something has viral potential? (You're probably asking yourself what the hell is viral potential?!

Viral potential is the latent ability that may be developed and lead to future virality or mass attraction on social media platforms.

Before posting anything on social media, considering its viral potential is always a must. Ask yourself the following questions and answer them in an unbiased manner.

How would I initially react to seeing this piece of content?

- Would I scroll past it?

- Would I like it?

- Would I share it with a friend or family member?

- Would I leave a comment? (If so what comment would I leave - we'll get more into this later)

Although it can be tough to be honest with yourself on something that you just spent hours creating, it's crucial to practice this exercise before posting if you are shooting for a viral piece of content.

The key takeaway from this is that value equates to virality. Make someone laugh, smile, or learn something and your chances of going viral are going to increase.

CHAPTER 8
STOP DOING WHAT EVERYONE ELSE IS DOING

"If you're doing what everyone else is doing, you're doing it wrong." - Casey Neistat

Every day I hear that the internet is saturated with creators and in some sense it's true. But honestly, this is just an excuse. If your niche is saturated, choose a different niche or create a niche inside your niche. The internet is never-ending and people are consuming content more and more EVERY SINGLE DAY.

I say "Stop Doing What Everyone Else is Doing" because it's tough to blow up on something that has ALREADY been done (and done to the best of its ability). Think of your 5 favorite creators that come to the top of your mind right now and think about why they are so successful in this industry. Did they just copy someone else or did they do something that

HAS NEVER BEEN DONE? Read that again… never been done.

Take these 5 creators for example:

- **Jimmy Donaldson (Mr. Beast):** Mr. Beast publicly reinvested every dollar of his YouTube earnings back into his over-the-top videos until he was extremely successful. He sacrificed every dollar he made to create some of the most entertaining content on the internet. From tipping strangers 10's of thousands of dollars to donating mass amounts of money to random twitch streamers, Mr. Beast's content is heavily original and this is one of the main reasons why he is so successful.

- **David Dobrik:** David Dobrik is known for his extremely fast-pace content where he films his best friends and just about everything they do for an entire week and only includes the best clips in a 4 minute and 20-second video. In the social media world, it's crucial to keep your audience hooked and

Dobrik does the absolute best job of this in his fast-paced exciting content.

- **Zach King:** Zach King made magic cool again. By using different online effects and editing strategies King built a massive personal brand around his internet magic videos.

- **Jake Paul:** Jake Paul initially rose to fame for his widely popular Team 10 content group. Paul was one of the first to create a house filled with influencers who would all collaborate and film videos on a daily. Although the house is no longer active, he pioneered the future for the social media world and other content collaboratives such as the Hype House and Sway House.

- **Daniel Mac:** Daniel Mac grew a massive following through his unique series of asking people what they do for a living. We've all seen an extremely expensive house or car and wondered what that person must do to make some serious money, but Daniel Mac's series got to the bottom of this.

If you want to blow up (and blow up FAST), you need to think of something so out of the box that hasn't been done before. Remember, the internet rewards you for your creativity. If you can curate a unique series of content that's unlike anything else, you're in good shape.

Wait, are you though? People come to me with AMAZING ideas every single day (seriously). But these people fail to execute on anything, they're all talk. They're the same people that laugh at Tik Tokers and say "anyone can do what they are doing, it's not that hard" but refuse to do it themselves. Being a content creator is NOT EASY. I know every other one is posting unrealistic pictures and making their lives out to be so lavish but that's far from the truth. Being creative 24/7 is hard and takes a toll on you.

CHAPTER 9
COMMENTS MEAN MORE THAN YOU THINK

"If you want to go viral, before you post anything on the internet, visualize and know exactly what the top comment will be." - Brendan Cox

You might think I'm crazy but comments are the reason why content goes viral on the internet. If you want to become a viral genius, throw in things in your videos that are BOUND to get the end-consumer to drop a comment. I call this "driving a top comment."

When you consume content (especially short-form content) do you just watch a video and scroll? NO. You don't... you watch a video and check the comments to see what's funny and relatable and like that comment.

Comments are the epitome of going viral and NO one talks about comments. You need an AMAZING comment section for your video to go viral. If it's just meh, the algorithm won't push your content out.

Take these 5 types of content for example: (If you aren't familiar with these types of videos I highly recommend doing a bit of research and digesting some of their content)

- **5 Minute Crafts:** Everyone thinks they are dumb but they are truly geniuses. 5 Minute Crafts make videos that are SO impractical that you have to drop a comment making fun of them. THIS is why every single one of their videos goes viral, think about it.

- **Rick Lax:** Rick Lax is an online entertainer known for his viral videos surrounding magic tricks. Best known on Facebook, Lax is the king of curating a viral comment section on his videos. From weird and confusing content and out-of-the-box tricks, Lax's ability to force users to leave a comment questioning the video is the main reason why he is so successful online.

How To Be Internet Famous

- **Jake Paul:** Influencer turned boxer is known for stirring the pot through his widely controversial videos. Wonder why? Because they drive comments! Whether you love him or hate him, you feel obliged to comment on all of his videos due to their outright insanity.

- **Trisha Paytas:** Trisha is one of the internet's longest-lasting creators but also one of the internet's most controversial people. Paytas jumps from one controversy to the next but in a genius way that keeps her relevant at all times. So many creators go in and out but Trisha will be around forever due to her ability to stir the pot and continually keep her comment section entertaining.

- **KeemStar:** Daniel Keem, best known on the internet as "KeemStar" runs the popular Influencer news show "DramaAlert." Keem jokes that he will never retire but I honestly believe him. He has a knack for internet drama and is constantly stirring up the drama on Twitter which drives retweets, comments, and non-stop banter from those who love him and those who despise him.

CHAPTER 10
TRIGGER ONE OF THE THREE TYPES OF EMOTIONAL EXPERIENCES

"Going viral isn't random, magic, or luck. It's a science." — Jonah Berger

Gaining virality has so much to do with an emotional experience on the other end of the screen.

Think to yourself: how is the person watching this video going to react?

- Are they going to laugh?

- Are they going to cry?

- Are they going to experience anger?

Emotional Experiences have three different components: a subjective experience, a physiological response, and a behavioral or expressive response.

Let's break these down:

Subjective Experience: Subjective experiences are those experiences which are unique to each person. The ways that individuals experience art, music and literature is subjective, which means it's different for everyone. Whether or not you like a certain work of art, song or book depends on your perception of it in relation to your own life situation and perspectives.

Physiological Response: A physiological response is a reaction to one or more of the five senses. These responses have been categorized by psychologists into three categories: excitatory, inhibitory and cognitive. For example, if an individual was in pain, they would exhibit an excitatory response such as flinching; whereas if they were exposed to something sour their body would exhibit a negative physiological response such as curling the lips - a common reaction to disgust.

Behavioral or Expressive Response: Behavioral or expressive response is the reaction that consumers have towards a stimulus. This can be an object, a person, an experience or even an emotion. In advertising and marketing, this refers to how a consumer responds to your advertising campaign.

The type of response will determine whether the campaign was successful or not, as well as what kind of follow-up actions you may wish to take.

It goes without saying that the three types of emotional experiences will create virality. Your content must be able to trigger an emotion, which should then lead to sharing your content with others through social media.

Brendan Cox

CHAPTER 11
KEEP UP WITH SOCIAL MEDIA TRENDS

"For those people who want to keep following trends, you do that and when the trend goes away so will you." - Ne-Yo

To have the best shot at becoming viral and staying relevant once you go viral, you need to keep up with social media in general. From new features to trends and more, social media is constantly changing, and keeping up with it is the research part of your job.

Let me be clear: DO NOT make your whole brand around a single trend as once that one trend ends so do you. BUT INSTEAD, consistently keep up with trends and stay in the loop with what's trending on the internet is key.

As a creator, you need to spend time on social media, sure for leisure but also to understand what's trending. The internet changes so fast so you only have so long to jump on a trend.

Brendan Cox

CHAPTER 12
KEYWORDS MATTER

Heard of SEO? If not, SEO stands for Search Engine Optimization and is an important thing to consider when your job is on the internet.

Have you ever wondered when you Google something, how Google chooses what information to feed you, and in what order? This is where SEO comes in. Search engine optimization is essentially the process of improving the amount and quality of website traffic you receive from search engines. Believe it or not, your YouTube videos and Instagram and Tik Tok posts are a part of this process. When you post a YouTube video, what keywords you use and the description of your video can dramatically impact the number of views your video gets.

MORE?

Brendan Cox

CHAPTER 13
SHORT & SWEET IS BETTER

On social media, one of the main aspects of every video-first social media platforms algorithm is watch time. Watch time, commonly referred to as audience retention is the total amount of time that viewers spend watching your content.

Why is watch time so important? Depending on how long your audience is watching your content lets the algorithms know how interesting your content is or how easily you can keep your audience hooked throughout your videos.

If on YouTube, a majority of your audience is only watching ⅓ of your video, clearly your content isn't engaging enough and therefore, YouTube's algorithm likely won't push out your video to others' recommended pages.

Analyzing statistics may seem tedious but doing so is crucial to understand your audience and what you are doing well and what you can improve on.

Brendan Cox

PART THREE

HOW TO BECOME "FAMOUS"

Brendan Cox

CHAPTER 14
DEFINING "FAME"

On a real note: what is fame? "Fame" is technically defined as "the state of being known or talked about by many people" which is fascinating because there are SO many more famous people today than there were 10 years ago. The internet has opened this wide lens into the life of hundreds of thousands of new 'content creators' that fall under the umbrella term of fame.

Brendan Cox

CHAPTER 15
KNOW EVERYONE AND THEIR MOTHER

If you haven't heard of the phrase "know everyone and their mother," now you do. The more people you know in the industry the better. Now when I say this I don't mean go slide in every famous person's DM's, but instead, try to create meaningful and most importantly authentic connections along your journey of becoming an influencer.

I consider myself a well-connected person. If you wanted to get in touch with a specific person (within reason) I genuinely believe it's not that difficult to get someone's attention. I've been able to get responses from almost everyone I've reached out to in the past 10 years (including billionaire Mark Cuban).

One of the most powerful things I've learned in life is that EVERYTHING and I mean EVERYTHING is about how you word things.

There are a few common misconceptions about connections and a lot of people (especially in this industry struggle to understand this). To connect with a high-level person you need to offer them some type of value. What can you do for them that will be of value to them? Anytime you want to get in touch with someone, ask yourself this.

If you are looking to get in touch with the CEO of a brand you're obsessed with: Explain how YOU can help THEM or give them some type of exposure on your platform.

So many (and I mean this) have this mixed up and reach out to people asking for favors and are bummed when they don't give them the time of day. To grab someone's attention you need to offer the initial value to make the connection.

CHAPTER 16
ASK FOR ADVICE AND FEEDBACK

Being afraid of asking for feedback is a thing of the past. As a creator bouncing ideas and content off of like-minded individuals is one of the best things to propel yourself to succeed.

You also need to be willing to ask for help and feedback. If your content is impressive, you'll want to continue posting it but there is always room for improvement. If you get more followers and likes, you'll feel a sense of validation that helps keep you going. But once your content starts to go viral, don't forget the humble beginnings of your social media career.

Ask other influencers or creators in a similar niche what they would do differently if they started from scratch. How can you improve? What mistakes did they make? What could you be doing more of? What should I stop doing?

If you get some good advice from people who inspire you, you'll get even better results eliminating those initial mistakes they might have made when starting out.

If you don't have friends in the social media space, don't hesitate to ask your audience for feedback. For example, if you want to know which of the two images is more appealing, leverage the Instagram polls feature to get a second opinion. Overall, DON'T be afraid to ASK, there is so much learning to be done in this constantly evolving space, and the more advice you get, the better.

CHAPTER 17
DIVERSIFY YOUR INCOME

The most popular social media influencers are those who have diversified their income streams. Almost every successful creator has multiple income streams, and when I say multiple, I don't mean 2 or 3, I mean over 10 different streams of revenue coming in regularly. Those that are killing it monetize all of their social networks and have created subtle business ventures around each of these platforms.

Monetizing your social media accounts is only going to become more important over time. Brands are beginning to recognize the value of influencer marketing, and are going to continue to want to work with influencers who can build brand awareness along with driving traffic and sales.

If you want to be successful as an influencer, you NEED to diversify your income streams. When one source of income dies or a platform is no longer around, it's crucial to have other ways to monetize your following. You can do this by conquering multiple social media platforms and building out different ways to make money from each (i'll get more into this later). When it comes to the best of the best of this industry, these creators do just that. Take Logan Paul for example. Logan owns Maverick Merchandise, Maverick Club, Prime (an energy drink) and has also been angel investing, just to name a few (the list goes on and on).

CHAPTER 18
WORK HARDER THAN EVERYONE ELSE

"Work like there is someone working 24 hours a day to take it all away from you."- Mark Cuban

Social media influencers are a dime a dozen. There's a new one popping up every day, and the sad reality is that most of them just get their 15 minutes of fame and then fall off.

The truth is, ANYONE can become an influencer and all it takes is time, consistency, and dedication. If you work harder than everyone else, you will achieve success in the social media space. While everyone else is scrolling on Tik Tok wasting 2 hours a day consuming comedic content, you should be making it. Everyone has the same 24 hours in a day, whether it's billionaire Warren Buffett or you. You also can't get discouraged if you don't go viral overnight. I've seen so many people give up so quickly in this industry and the people that are winning are always the ones that just never stop creating (regardless of the views, followers and likes). You need to know your audience's wants and needs, identify your true passion, and have a realistic expectation of your results. You can't expect to start seeing results right away, but you do need to be willing to put in the time and effort to earn the authority to speak on behalf of your brand.

CHAPTER 19
LEARN HOW TO ADAPT

If there is one thing that is clear about this space, it's that it changes just about every day. From trends to new in-app features to completely new platforms, it can get overwhelming. As a creator, you need to pick your shots and focus on a few things at once. Trying to do it all will almost always lead to burnout, especially in this space where the lines are blurred between what is and isn't working.

The best way to do this is by adapting. With the nature of this social media space, successful apps are constantly implementing new features and tools that sometimes are great and sometimes absolutely suck.

At the end of the day, you need to be constantly adapting and willing to CHANGE if you want to succeed in this space.

Brendan Cox

CHAPTER 20
IT'S NOT ROCKET SCIENCE

"The greatest ideas are the simplest."- William Golding

If you're a beginner with zero followers on social media, this might sound like an insult but the truth is, social networks are designed for everyone to be able to use them and grow.

To go from zero followers to a thousand in a short time frame takes a lot of hard work and dedication, but it's possible. You must be willing to put your time into growing your personal brand.

You also need to have great content that is appealing enough for potential followers who are going to engage with what you are putting out. Remember that these are REAL people watching your videos. These are not bots (of course some are) but generally there are REAL people on the other side of the screen consuming your content. So next time you are creating your content, think about what type of videos your viewers would want to consume. Let them know you have their interest in mind without telling them you do.

PART FOUR

MONETIZING YOUR REACH

Brendan Cox

CHAPTER 21
FOLLOWERS DON'T EQUATE TO MONEY

One of the biggest challenges for influencers is monetizing their followings. Getting the initial viral video can be a piece of cake for some people but turning their influence into a full time job is the difficult part. There are various ways to do this, but many influencers make the mistake of associating monetary success directly with followers. The truth is that even in a saturated market, people can be drawn to you if your personality shines through and they have a genuine desire to engage with you. It's important to understand that followers DO NOT equate to money. I've seen creators with 5 million followers struggle to score a $1,000 brand deal, while some micro-influencers with 25,000 followers post a $1,000 brand deal every week. It's all about how you sell yourself and how well you can integrate brands into your audience.

Essentially what I am trying to say is that STOP CARING ABOUT FOLLOWERS. Yes, I know it sounds twisted and dumb in this "numbers" driven industry but if there is one statistic to look at its engagement. If you can create a really tight niche community that LOVES and ENGAGES with your content, then you are golden.

CHAPTER 22
MAKE BRANDS WANT YOU

MAKE BRANDS WANT YOU. It's literally that simple. If you can create a presence that is brand-friendly, you are in AMAZING shape.

What does being "brand-friendly" mean? No, this doesn't always mean no curse words, family friendly, etc (although it often does help). Being brand-friendly essentially means your content is really easy to incorporate brands into in a nonchalant way.

Take a look at Emily Zugay for example. Zugay started a Tik Tok series where she would make "redesigns" of various company logos like; Microsoft, Tik Tok, and so on. Her content is brand-friendly, which captivates the attention of various brands to her "redesigns".

There's a lot of money (due to huge corporate influencer marketing budgets) to be made in the world of social media influencers. Brands are more and more willing to pay for influencer-created content that will appeal to their target market.

That's where you come in with a MASSIVE VALUE ADD for these brands. Create something that is so valuable for them that they will feel dumb turning it down. Whether it's super high-quality content that they can repurpose for ad content or they can also post it to their other social channels.

The key is to work with these brands to identify the perfect campaign and build mutually beneficial relationships that will resonate with their audiences.

Building your brand is hard work and takes time. But as you start to gain more exposure and your content starts gaining traction, brands will come knocking on your door looking for you to partner with them.

CHAPTER 23
DON'T PROMOTE GARBAGE

Before promoting a company to your audience, you should investigate thoroughly what type of brand it is. Don't promote scams or shady companies that you know nothing about. Remember your fans are real people and they look up to you. Diligently perform a thorough background check of every brand that you have the opportunity to work with. It sounds too good to be true, it probably is.

Because of the nature of this fast-paced industry, you might end up promoting products are a headache. Sometimes, you won't know much about what you're promoting until after you've committed to it, which is when it's usually too late to back out without tarnishing your reputation in social media.

If you're thinking about following in the footsteps of one of your favorite social media influencers, think again. It's easy to fall for a bad product or brand that you've seen promoted by someone else and ignore all the red flags. You might end up wasting time and even money on collaborations that don't work or end up hurting your credibility with your followers.

So how do you avoid these issues? Here are 3 tips to make sure you only work with credible products and brands:

Tip #1: Read online reviews before endorsing a company

There are hundreds of reviews online for every major brand out there, from cars to beauty products and anything in between. You can easily find them for any product or service, and you should do so before signing any contracts.

Tip #2: Don't be afraid to turn down offers from brands you can't recommend

There's a lot to consider here. It's hard to say no to money, but when you promote something, and your followers don't like it, you're setting yourself up for failure. There are plenty of brands out there that will compensate you for a sponsored project and whose products live up to the hype - go with one of those instead.

Tip #3: Be completely transparent with your followers

Exonerate yourself from future scandals by keeping it real with your followers. Be completely transparent with them about everything and not only will they be more likely to support brands you promote but they will be more likely to engage with your content that shows an authentic version of yourself.

Brendan Cox

CHAPTER 24
KNOW YOUR WORTH

When you are trying to make a name for yourself in the social media community, it is important to understand what you have to offer and how much that can be worth. In order to successfully market yourself as a social media influencer, you will need to come up with fair rates that take into account the entire scope of your business. Social media has given everyone the power to reach a global audience. But it also gives anyone the opportunity to share their opinions, ideas, and content with hundreds of thousands of people just by posting something on social media. As brands now turn to social influencers for promotion, how do you know your worth as an influencer? How do you increase your value? Connecting with influencers is always a good way to find the "going rate" for certain promotions.

Remember, If you want to become a full-time social media influencer, you have bills to pay too. Is it reasonable for someone to pay you $100 per post? $1,000? Or $10,000?

What I always tell my clients is that you are WAY better off taking less, higher paying brand deals than spamming your socials with a bunch of low-paying integrations.

Two key takeaways: One: don't be afraid to say NO to low-ball offers. Two: Everything in this industry is negotiable, if someone offers you $5,000 for a brand deal, it can't hurt asking for an extra $1,000.

I'll never forget the time I negotiated a $2,000 brand deal up to $14,000 with a single email (yes ONE single email 7X the price of the brand deal).

CHAPTER 25
WAYS TO MONETIZE

Built your audience and now ready to make some dough? These days, most people with even a modest following on social media can earn money through advertising, sponsored posts, affiliate marketing, and a handful of other monetization strategies.

Working in the influencer marketing space for years, there are so many unique ways to make money that I never realized. Here are just SOME of your monetization options and how I've helped many influencers ace each of them:

BRAND INTEGRATIONS

Brand integrations are the process of brands partnering with digital influencers to essentially share their products or services amongst these creators' audiences. Typically, YOU the influencer creates an original post showcasing the brand's product or service in a unique way.

One example of a typical brand integration is the partnership between Ice-T and Friskies. The rapper posted a picture of himself with a bowl of Friskies food, sponsored by Friskies. The picture showed the Lil' Chunks cat food brand sponsored by Friskies. The rapper also included their social media handles at the end of the post.

Brand deals are the most common way that influencers (especially micro-influencers) earn a living. Creators such as the Kardashians rake in over $1 million for a single Instagram post. Yes, you read that correctly: $1 million dollars. Other great examples are Mike Krieger and Kaitlyn Alexander, who have been paid absurd amounts of money to promote companies such as Airbnb.

This style of marketing is here to stay, as people put trust into influencers to showcase products and services that would be beneficial to their audiences. The ad industry is shifting more and more towards influencer marketing as companies target young consumers who are used to more intrusive ads. Brands are also leveraging this style of marketing to reach out to influencers' young, tech-savvy audiences by pushing out their brands across these influencers' social media channels.

Why are these partnerships so popular amongst influencers? Influencers and brands that come together in a unique way like this can make both parties happy (what I like to call a WIN WIN). The influencers get compensated to promote brands that they're interested in (and of course get some freebies) while brands get to reach an audience they wouldn't have been able to reach otherwise.

Brand integrations are an excellent way for companies to partner with influencers to guarantee that their product will be seen and gain brain recognition online. The companies can also subtly advertise their products by including them in the regular day-to-day content of the influencers they partner with. This type of marketing is often more appealing to young people than more conventional forms of advertising, like commercials and billboards, since it doesn't seem invasive or obvious.

AFFILIATE MARKETING

If you've always had the entrepreneur mindset, "I don't want to work for somebody else; I want to do my own thing!" then affiliate marketing could be a great extra stream of income for you.

What is affiliate marketing? Essentially affiliate marketing is the process of acting as an intermediary between a company, the affiliate, and someone who wants to buy their product or service, the consumer. If the consumer decides that they would like to buy something after seeing your post about it, you (the promoter) will get a commission. This is just turning your social media followers into customers - all businesses need customers, so they are always looking for ways of bridging that gap.

Social media influencers with strong niche followings are the perfect candidates for affiliate marketing because they already have a dedicated fan base surrounding a certain topic. If you find the correct (and on-brand) products and services to promote, it's like throwing a piece of jewelry into a pool full of fish. With an already established following, the business will come to you.

As with any business, it pays to diversify your revenue stream and balance the risk across several sources. Affiliate marketing is one way that social media influencers can diversify their revenue streams and earn some extra money passively by promoting products and/or services.

Let's break down the different ways to earn money through affiliate marketing:

1. One-to-One sales: Post about a product or service that you know would be of value to your audience, and people will click through to the site, buy it, and you'll earn a commission.

2. Product reviews: Posting a review of certain products on your socials is a great way to show off cool and trendy products and make an extra buck when your followers decide to purchase by using your link. Many websites have affiliate programs designed to drive traffic back to the site through social media influencers. These affiliate programs can vary from a humble 5% commission for each sale to 50%, depending on the product or service for sale.

One prime example is using Amazon's affiliate program. You can literally promote anything on Amazon and earn a commission for each sale you get.

The amount of money you can make as a social media influencer through affiliate marketing depends on numerous factors, including how many followers your account has, how often you post and what kind of products or services you are promoting, and how much of a commission you earn per sale.

The affiliate marketing industry is very promising, and it will be a part of the future social media and online shopping for years to come. As a social media influencer, you have the opportunity to grow your revenue stream by becoming an affiliate marketing expert by scoping out on-brand products that will be lucrative in the long run.

BUILDING OUT YOUR OWN PRODUCTS

Another common way creators earn a living is by building out their own products. An extreme example is Kylie Jenner and her insanely popular Kylie Cosmetics brand. It's becoming more and more common for celebrities and influencers of all sizes to curate their own line of products branded under their name.

This is definitely a more time consuming route as you are either partnering with a current company and white labeling or you are creating your own brand from scratch. Here are a few tips to get you started:

1. Perform market research to understand the market you are targeting.

You should understand your target audience and research their wants and needs. It also helps if you understood what challenges your followers might be going through and bringing value to them with your products. For example if you are an influencer surrounding the fitness niche, you may have a product or service in mind that will assist people in losing weight.

2. Stay on-brand and authentic

Make sure to align yourself with a product that is relevant to your target demographic. One of the biggest mistakes people make is creating what I like to call "money grabs." People can tell when you are just doing something for quick money rather then because it's a project you are genuinely passionate about.

3. Leverage social media

After you launch your product, leverage your fan base to market future products on social media. Whether that means starting an ambassador

How To Be Internet Famous

program, or offering exclusive discounts and deals only available to those who follow you, there are so many ways to leverage social media in building your business.

4. Use systems and tools such as email marketing to build your audience.

When building your brand, use services such as Mailchimp or Telligent Mailer to create email newsletters that provide an easy way of promoting new products and giving updates on what is happening with your business. You should also make sure that you stay on top of the latest trends by reading up on your niche, even if it is something that you have no interest in personally.

5. Create content to keep bringing in new followers

Remember people DON'T have to follow you. Because of this, you need to give people a reason why they SHOULD follow, and support you. This can be as simple as giving information about your upcoming products or special deals exclusively for people who follow you.

Make sure that your content is interesting and relevant for your audience. It is important to emphasize why they should trust what you have to say about a product or service.

LIVE STREAMING

Live streaming is becoming a more and more prominent way to earn a living on the internet. Many of the platforms that allow live streaming are free to use and offer unique advantages, but there are also some limitations in terms of monetization. Social media influencers are typically able to monetize their content by having fans watch ads or charging for pre-recorded videos before live streaming. So, if you're an influencer who has an addictive personality and can talk for hours, then live streaming might just be your thing.

Streaming lets users live-stream a video to their followers in real-time. It is a tool for regular people and organizations, including brands and companies, to broadcast live video. In general, live streaming is the process of watching or listening to a video presented by another person from another location without being in the same place as the presenter. People usually use live streaming for online training, education or (most commonly amongst influencers) for entertainment.

There are several platforms for live streaming. Here's a breakdown of the most popular streaming platforms:

Meerkat: Meerkat is a live streaming app that lets users stream directly to their followers. Compared to Twitch, it's easier for users to discover content and interact with other viewers through Meerkat's chat feature. It also offers setting up alerts, live streaming from an individual or channel, playing music, and more.

Twitch: Twitch is one of the most popular social media platforms that allow users to live stream video games. It was first launched in 2011 and has become the core of internet culture and video game culture, particularly among video gamers. One of the benefits of Twitch is that it allows users to set up private streams and run advertisements during the stream. This means that [Influencers] can push out a limited number of ads for their fans to watch during live streaming.

YouTube Live: YouTubers often stream their lives with other platforms, but YouTube also allows users to professionally bring in a crowd and make money through live streaming. Using this platform, one can create a live stream broadcast focused on their streamers and utilize some of YouTube's tools to achieve their goals, increase their viewership and boost sales.

Like Twitch and Meerkat, YouTube Live allows influencers to monetize their viewers. There are two types of subscriptions available on this platform. The first is a free tier where influencers can only broadcast once every 24 hours. The second subscription is the paid subscription, where users must place ads before or during the live stream.

Facebook Live: Facebook Live is another popular streaming option that can be used for the same purpose as other platforms such as Twitch, YouTube, and Meerkat. One of the best features of Facebook Live is that it allows users to earn from their video content through an ad break. This means an influencer earns money every time a user views or clicks an ad on their live stream.

Many of the platforms that allow live streaming are free to use and offer unique advantages, but there are also some limitations in terms of monetization. In summary, pushing out ads in between streams or charging for pre-recorded videos is typically the biggest way streamers earn money.

How do social media influencers monetize paid content with Facebook's ad breaks?

Back in March 2016, Facebook introduced the paid video creators platform, which was referred to as Facebook Watch at the time. This platform is different from original programming since it's designed for content creators and not established television networks. For example, one can upload videos on Facebook Watch and make money from advertisements while live streaming on the platform.

The main advantage of using this platform is that it allows influencers to have better control of their revenue by choosing which ads they want to run on their live streams and monetizing their video content through the ad breaks.

BRAND CONSULTING

Before I began working behind the scenes of influencers I had no idea how much money companies would pay influencers for their opinion. When companies see someone with thousands of followers in a certain niche, they often want feedback and advice on how to best optimize their social presence to be set up for success. In consulting brands, influencers can earn money by simply lending their voice and feedback to various companies. In other words, as an influencer your "voice" and "opinion" is valued highly by companies and there are certain surveys, focus groups and virtual calls where you can make some serious money just by speaking up!

SELLING A COURSE OR DIGITAL PRODUCT

In this digital era we are living in, selling a course or digital product is one of the easiest and most lucrative businesses that influencers are in. Digital products are excellent extra streams of income to add to your portfolio as they are heavily passive. Once you spend the initial time building out your course or digital product, all you have to do is promote it.

Whether you create a social media course or an e-book focused on a niched down topic (like KETO recipes for example), the market for digital products is only going to continue to get bigger and bigger over time.

SPEAKING AT EVENTS

High schools and universities are realizing more and more the power that these social media influencers have on the world. What used to just be a viral Tik

Toker is now someone who can get hired at any Fortune 500 company as the head of their marketing department.

Therefore, more and more schools are inviting (whether it be virtually or in person) influencers to speak to their students and educate them of the vast world of social media. Universities in particular have huge event budgets built into tuitions for speakers just like this.

If you enjoy talking about social media and think this could be a fit for you, put together an amazing media kit and start pitching school's exactly what you have to offer!

How To Be Internet Famous

CHAPTER 26
DON'T OVERTHINK IT

The number one thing I notice about wannabe social media influencers is that so many people overthink everything. Is there an ideal time to post? Should I buy followers? Should I use 3 hashtags or 4 hashtags? Should I wait until Sunday to post? Should I not post at all? Should I tag her in the picture or in the caption?

STOP OVERTHINKING IT. Remember, on the other side of the internet is real people looking to consume content that brings them value. If you bring value and post quality content, you are on track to succeed. Don't let the little things like posting times and hashtags distract you from the more important things.

All in all, you got this. I truly believe anyone can achieve success as a creator online if you implement the advice I gave you in this book and put in the time and effort. As Jake Paul once said, you gotta want it.

ACKNOWLEDGMENTS

Thank you, thank you, thank you to everyone who had some part in this book or my social media journey - but especially to:

My family: who since day one has believed in me and supported me through everything I have done.

My friends: Devin, Lauren, Abraham, Evan, Spencer, Eli & so many others. Whether we've been friends for 10 years or I just met you this year, I appreciate your constant support and guidance on this unique social media journey I have set out on.

My followers: I'm just kidding, I don't have many (remember, I don't like being in the spotlight) but maybe we should change that? Feel free to connect with me on Instagram @BrendanACox.

Printed in Great Britain
by Amazon